CHECK YOUR ORDER!!!

Angela McMillan Johnson

CHECK YOUR ORDER
Copyright © 2021 by Angela McMillan Johnson

All rights reserved. No part of this publication may be reproduced, distributed, or transmitted in any form or by any means, including photocopying, recording, or other electronic or mechanical methods, without the prior written permission of the publisher or author, except in the case of brief quotations embodied in critical reviews and certain other noncommercial uses permitted by copyright law.

Although every precaution has been taken to verify the accuracy of the information contained herein, the author and publisher assume no responsibility for any errors or omissions. No liability is assumed for damages that may result from the use of information contained within.

Library of Congress Control Number: 2021914930
ISBN-13:   Paperback: 978-1-64749-566-4

Printed in the United States of America

GoTo Publish

GoToPublish LLC
1-888-337-1724
www.gotopublish.com
info@gotopublish.com

CHECK YOUR ORDER!!!

What You Say Is What You Get

Thank God for Jesus!!!

**His intercession keeps us alive and gives numberless chances to get it right.
Romans 8:34**

To GOD Be The Glory!

AJ

DEDICATION

William and Mary Harden
for laying the foundation for our family.

Husband, Johnny, for encouraging me to not say, "I can't do this". Son, Geoffrey, daughter, Danielle, for praising my every effort. Granddaughter, Jessica, for telling me that I am "all that". Grandson Daniel for his hugs and kisses.

Pastor <u>Rich</u>ard P. Harden for imparting his wisdom, encouragement, and blessing for the project.
Prophetess Irell Harden and her perfect example of discipleship.

Mother, Omie Ruth McMillan, for putting up with my nonsense and loving me anyway

Siblings; Sondra, Chevie, Michael, for always being there for me.

Friends: Marita, Carol, Phyllis, Pat, Brenda, for having my back for any project.

All other family and friends for their prayers for me always.

In Memoriam

William Harden

Mary Harden

Omie Ruth McMillan

Pat Range

Sondra Byrd

Carol Cook

Irell Harden

Ж

Unless otherwise stated,
Scripture references
taken from
New King James Version

Copyright © 1994
by Thomas Nelson , Inc.
Used by permission.
All rights reserved.

Photos and text, by author,
are initialed, all others
are obtained from
public domain. (internet)

Chapters

1. And It Was So...　　　　　　　　20
   Creation

2. Who He Is　　　　　　　　　　　32
   The Essence of God

3. Purpose and Value　　　　　　　46
   The Word of God

4. Blessed and Cursed　　　　　　72
   The Power of What We Say

5. Faith Works　　　　　　　　　　86
   Only Believe

6. The Consequences of Unbelief　106
   What It Does To Us

7. Redeemed by His Blood　　　　112
   Through His Word

8. Who This Works For　　　　　　126
   Who "Gets" It

9. How to Receive　　　　　　　　132
   What About Me?

10. What Now?　　　　　　　　　　142
    Where Do I Go From Here?

Scripture References　　　　　　　156
Cover Girl　　　　　　　　　　　　158

While praying once, God said to me, "Pray My Word, Speak My Word, Stand on My Word. For, just like a tree planted by the water, I shall not be moved. "

His Word is true and everlasting.
He is not a man that He should lie.

Ж

Your Word is a lamp to my feet and a light to my path.

Psalm 119:105

God is our Creator. He identifies Himself as I AM THAT I AM; that sentient being that was and is and is to come, who is Omnitent, Omniscient, Omnipresent. He is the great Three In One. The Father, the Son, and the Holy Ghost; the Triune Spirit. He is our Father, our Banner, our Provider, Ruler of all Creation.

Through His Son, He is our Savior, the Anointed One, King of Kings and Lord of Lords. He is the Alpha and Omega—The Beginning and the End. He bought our Salvation; through Him, we live and breathe.

Through His Holy Spirit, He is the Sweet Heavenly Dove, Precious Holy Ghost, who sanctifies, edifies, comforts, keeps, teaches, and guides us. He leads us into all truths; grants us righteousness, peace, and joy, wisdom, knowledge, and understanding. He speaks to us, for us, and through us.

God grants us favor with all men. He supplies our every need. He encamps His angels round about us to keep us safe from all hurt, harm and danger.

God loves us in spite of ourselves. He is patient, caring, strong and mighty.

AJ

The greatest purpose of man, is to glorify God. "Therefore, whether you eat or drink, or whatever you do, do all to the glory of God.   (**1 Corinthians 10:31**).

Glorifying God requires knowledge of God and knowing Him personally in view of that knowledge.   paraphrased **Robert Lightner,   *The God of the Bible, An Introduction to the Doctrine of God* (Baker Book House, Grand Rapids, 1973)**

Have you ever heard anyone say this?

"That will never happen."
"I can't do that."
"They are just like their no-good father and mother."
"I get sick every year at this time."
"I will never have any money."
"I'm not smart enough to do that."
"Why should I think that anything will change, It's always *been* that way. It will always *be* that way."
"I am going to die with this."
"You know when you get that, you're going to die. It's incurable. "
"But the doctor said it's inoperable."
 (Every word a curse)

Think before you speak, you may have to eat those words, or at least ...live them.

The darkness that our words produce.

And It Was So...

Ж

Creation

In the beginning, God created the heavens and the earth.

Genesis 1:1, 3, 6, 9, 13, 14, 20, 24, 26, 28, 30

> And *God said,* Let there be light, and there was light.

> And *God said,* Let there be a firmament in the midst of the waters and let it divide the waters from the waters which were above the firmament and it was so,

> And *God said,* Let the waters under the heavens be gathered together unto one place, and let the dry ground appear, and it was so.

And *God said*, Let the earth bring forth grass, the herb that yields seed, and the fruit tree that yields fruit according to its kind, whose seed is in itself, on the earth, and it was so,

And *God said*, Let there be lights in the firmament of the heaven to divide the day from the night, and let them be for signs and seasons, and for days, and for years.

And *God said*, Let the waters abound with an abundance of living creatures, and let birds fly above the earth across the face of the firmament of the heavens.

<u>And *God said,*</u> Let the earth bring forth the living creature according to its kind, cattle and creeping things and beasts of the earth after his kind, *<u>and it was so</u>*.

Also to every beast of the earth, to every bird of the air, and to everything that creeps on the earth, in which there is life, I have given every green herb for food,", <u>and it was so.</u>

Genesis 1:26-31 <u>Then God said,</u> "Let Us make man in Our image, according to Our likeness; let them have dominion over the fish of the sea, over the birds of the air, and over the cattle, over all the earth and over every creeping thing that creeps on the earth."

So God created man in His *own* image; in the image of God He created him; male and female He created them.

Then God blessed them, and <u>God said</u> to them, "Be fruitful and multiply; fill the earth and subdue it; have dominion over the fish of the sea, over the birds of the air, and over every living thing that moves on the earth."

<u>And God said</u>, "See, I have given you every herb that yields seed which *is* on

the face of all the earth, and every tree whose fruit yields seed; to you it shall be for food.

Also, to every beast of the earth, to every bird of the air, and to everything that creeps on the earth, in which *there is* life, *I have given* every green herb for food"; <u>and it was so.</u>

Then God saw everything that He had made, and indeed *it was* very good. So the evening and the morning were the sixth day.

Genesis 2:1-4   Thus the heavens and the earth, and all the host of them, were finished.

And on the seventh day God ended His work which He had done, and He rested

Then God blessed the seventh day and sanctified it, because in it He rested from all His work which God had created and made.

This *is* the history of the heavens and the earth when they were created, in the day that the LORD GOD made the earth and the heavens.

God's creation plan included the beginning of mankind. He formed man from the dust of the earth. From nothing came a great creation. God breathed the breath of life into man, making man a part of Himself.

Our lives are attached to Him and cannot be separated. We resist, we rebel, but cannot completely remove ourselves from our Creator. Submitting brings such power but we think it makes us weak.

A king's children are heirs to his throne. Thus, they have access to all the king's treasures. God says the cattle on a thousand hills belong to Him. The streets of Heaven are paved with gold. What treasures there are for His children!?

Disobedient children get nothing from a responsible parent, except discipline and love. God is the ultimate parent.

Parents that reward bad behaviors are not doing their child any favors. It will all catch up with the child and the parents some day. When we reward bad behavior, The child expects that all the time and the actions get worse as they get older.

The real world cares nothing about your child being cute or smart. There are millions just like yours. God says do not support bad behaviors. He does not support our bad behaviors, but rewards our obedience with everything we need to prosper.

$\boxed{AJ}$

III John 2   Beloved, I pray that you may prosper in all things and be in health, just as your soul prospers.

Who HE Is

Ж

The Essence of God

There are many names used in reference to God. Following are a few:

Abba: Abba is Aramaic in origin, but the Hebrew's use it to refer to **Father or Daddy** when referring to God. They choose to use Abba because it describes their close, personal relationship with God (Mark 14:36; Rom. 8:15; Gal. 4:6).

Elohim: **Strong One**, it stresses majesty and intimates the Trinity. It is especially used of God's sovereignty, creative work, mighty work for Israel and in relation to His sovereignty (Isa. 54:5; Jer. 32:27; Gen. 1:1; Isa. 45:18; Deut. 5:23; 8:15; Ps. 68:7).

El Shaddai: "God Almighty." God's loving supply and comfort; His power as the Almighty one standing on a mountain and who corrects and chastens (Gen. 17:1; 28:3; 35:11; Ex. 6:1; Ps. 91:1, 2).

El Elyon: "The Most High God." Stresses God's strength, sovereignty, and supremacy (Gen. 14:19; Ps. 9:2; Dan. 7:18, 22, 25).

El Olam: "The Everlasting God." Emphasizes God's unchangeableness and is connected with His inexhaustibleness (Gen. 16:13).

Yahweh (YHWH): Comes from a verb which means "to exist, be." This, plus its usage, shows that this name stresses God as the independent and self-existent God of revelation and redemption (Gen. 4:3; Ex. 6:3 (cf. 3:14); 3:12).

Yahweh Maccaddeshcem: "The Lord your Sanctifier." Portrays the Lord as our means of sanctification or as the one who sets believers apart for His purposes (Ex. 31:13).

Yahweh Ro'i*:* "The Lord my Shepherd." Portrays the Lord as the Shepherd who cares for His people as a shepherd cares for the sheep of his pasture (Ps. 23:1).

Yahweh Jireh (Yireh): "The Lord will provide." Stresses God's provision for His people (Gen. 22:14).

Yahweh Nissi: "The Lord is my Banner." Stresses that God is our rallying point and our means of victory; the one who fights for His people (Ex. 17:15).

Yahweh Shalom: "The Lord is Peace." Points to the Lord as the means of our peace and rest (Jud. 6:24).

Yahweh Shammah: "The Lord is there." Portrays the Lord's personal presence in the millennial kingdom (Ezek. 48:35).

Yahweh Sabbaoth: "The Lord of Hosts." A military figure portraying the Lord as the commander of the armies of Heaven (1 Sam. 1:3; 17:45).

Yahweh Tsidkenu: "The Lord our Righteousness." Portrays the Lord as the means of our righteousness (Jer. 23:6).

Yahweh Elohim Israel: "The Lord, the God of Israel." Identifies Yahweh as the God of Israel in contrast to the false gods of the nations (Jud. 5:3.; Isa. 17:6).

Adonai: Like *Elohim*, this too is a plural of majesty. The singular form means "Master, Owner." Stresses man's relationship to God as his master, authority, and provider (Gen. 18:2; 40:1; 1Sam. 1:15; Ex. 21:1-6; Josh. 5:14).

Theos: Greek word translated "God." Primary name for God used in the New Testament. Its use teaches: (1) *He is the only true God* (Matt. 23:9; Rom. 3:30); (2) *He is unique* (1 Tim. 1:17; John 17:3; Rev. 15:4; 16:7); (3) *He is transcendent* (Acts 17:24; Heb. 3:4; Rev. 10:6); (4) *He is the Savior* (John 3:16; 1 Tim. 1:1; 2:3; 4:10). This name is used of Christ as God in John 1:1,18; 20:28; 1 John 5:20; Tit. 2:13; Rom. 9:5; Heb.1:8; 2 Pet. 1:1.

Kurios: Greek word translated "Lord." Stresses authority and supremacy. While it can mean Sir (John 4:11), owner (Luke 19:33), master (Col. 3:22), or even refer to idols (1 Cor. 8:5) or husbands (1 Pet. 3:6), It is used mostly as the equivalent of *Yahweh* of the Old Testament. It, too, is used of Jesus Christ meaning (1) Rabbi or Sir (Matt. 8:6); (2) God or Deity (John 20:28; Acts 2:36; Rom. 10:9; Phil. 2:11).

***Despotes*:** Greek word translated "Master." Carries the idea of ownership while *Kurios* stressed supreme authority (Luke 2:29; Acts 4:24; Rev. 6:10; 2 Pet. 2:1; Jude 4).

***Father*:** A distinctive New Testament revelation is that, through faith in Christ, God becomes our "Personal Father". Father is used of God in the Old Testament only 15 times while it is used of God 245 times in the New Testament. As a name of God, it stresses God's loving care, provision, discipline, and the way we are to address God in prayer (Matt. 7:11; Jam. 1:17; Heb. 12:5-11; John 15:16; 16:23; Eph.2:18; 3:15; 1 Thess. 3:11).

Robert Lightner, *The God of the Bible*
An Introduction to the Doctrine of God
(Baker Book House, Grand Rapids, 1973)

There are a number of instances where no name of God is employed, but where simply the term "name" in reference to God is used as the point of focus:

(1) Abraham called on the *name* of the Lord (Gen. 12:8; 13:4).

(2) The Lord proclaimed His own *name* before Moses (Ex. 33:19; 34:5).

(3) Israel was warned against profaning the *name* of the Lord (Lev. 13:21; 22:2, 32).

(4) The *name* of the Lord was not to be taken in vain (Ex. 20:7; Deut. 5:11).

(5) The priests of Israel were to minister in the *name* of the Lord (Deut. 18:5; 21:5).

(6) The *name* of God is called "wonderful" in (Judges 13:18).

(7) To call on the *name* of the Lord was to worship Him as God (Gen. 21:33; 26:25).

(8) It is at the *name* of Jesus that every knee will one day bow and every tongue confess that Jesus Christ is Lord (Phil. 2:10-11).

So, just as the name of God in the Old Testament spoke of the holy character of God the Father, so the name of Jesus in the New Testament speaks of the holy character of God, the Son.

Consequently, from this we can conclude that such phrases as "the name of the LORD" or "the name of God" refer to God's whole character. It was a summary statement embodying the entire person of God. When we turn to the New Testament we find the same. The name of Jesus is used in a similar way to the name of God in the Old Testament: Salvation is through His *name*

(1) But as any as received Him, gave he power to become sons of God, even to them that believe on His name. (John 1:12).

(2) Believers are to gather in His *name* (Matt. 18:20).

(3) Prayer is to be made in His *name* (John 14:13-14).

(4) The servant of the Lord who bears the *name* of Christ will be hated (Matt. 10:22).

(5) The book of Acts makes frequent mention of worship, service, and suffering in the *name* of Jesus Christ. Acts 4:18; 5:28, 41; 10:43; 19:17).

Acts 5:38 "Did we not strictly command you not to teach in this *name*? And look, you have filled Jerusalem with your doctrine, and intend to bring this Man's blood on us!"

So they departed from the presence of the council, rejoicing that they were counted worthy to suffer shame for His *name*.

To Him all the prophets witness that, through His *name*, whoever believes in Him will receive remission of sins."

This became known both to all Jews and Greeks dwelling in Ephesus; and fear fell on them all, and the *name* of the Lord Jesus was magnified.

Romans 11:33-36 Oh, the depth of the riches both of the wisdom and knowledge of God! How unsearchable *are* His judgments and His ways past finding out!

" For who has known the mind of the LORD?
Or who has become His counselor?"
" Or who has first given to Him
And it shall be repaid to him?"

For of Him and through Him and to Him *are* all things, to whom *be* glory forever.

Amen.

Robert Lightner, *The God of the Bible, An Introduction to the Doctrine of God* (Baker Book House, Grand Rapids, 1973)

Purpose and Value

Ж

The Word of God

I read in the Bible, once or twice, actually, several times, that we should "go into all the world and preach the gospel." I said to myself, "that doesn't apply to me. There are lots of people who like doing that sort of thing; I'll support them, they're good at it." But, I knew that I was just fooling myself. I know that all commands and promises are for all of us.

But the enemy said, "Who do you think you are?" He reminded me of all my past mistakes and shortcomings. Of course, he didn't know that I had just submitted myself to God.

And just then, God whispered in my ear, "Remember who you are." He reminded me that I am a child of God, washed in the blood of the lamb. A new creature in Christ Jesus. Old things are passed away, all things have become new. I have the mind of Christ and am in Christ, seated at the right hand of the Father. He told me that I am a joint heir with Christ Jesus; so, with Him, I have been granted authority over all things.

The weapons of my warfare are not carnal but mighty through God to the pulling down of strongholds. I am able to cast down imaginations and every high thing that exalts itself against the knowledge of God and bring into captivity every thought to the obedience of Christ.

I am more than a conqueror through Christ Jesus; for greater is He that is in me than He that is in the world. I am what He says I am.

I am the salt of the earth, I am a sheep in His pasture, a peculiar person, having been chosen by God through my acceptance of Christ Jesus as my personal savior.

I am blessed and highly favored, a king and a priest, a *god,* according to Christ Jesus. I am made in the spiritual image of the most-high God. I overcome all things through the blood of the Lamb and the word of my testimony. I am strong in the Lord and the power of His might.

I know that there is nothing I can go through that He isn't in. I know that there is no place He will send me that He hasn't gone before me to prepare the way. I know that He has prepared me and given me all that I need to do His will.

God waits on me to come to Him, because He loves me. He waits on me to speak His Word because He listens for His Word to perform it. He hastens His Word to accomplish its task. His Word does not return to Him empty having not accomplished its goal.

I know that I eat from the fruit of my mouth. I bridle my tongue and guard my words to eat bountifully by speaking His Word over my children, over my family, over my life. I know that He will do exceedingly abundantly above what I can ask or even think. I am what He says I am.

I give Him all honor, praise and glory. Hallelujah!

AJ

Proverbs 2:1-12 My son, if you receive My words, and treasure My commands within you, So that you incline your ear to wisdom, and apply your heart to understanding;

Yes, if you cry out for discernment,
And lift up your voice for understanding,

If you seek her as silver, and search for her as for hidden treasure;

Then you will understand the fear of the Lord, and find the knowledge of God.

For the Lord gives wisdom; from His mouth comes knowledge and understanding;

He stores up sound wisdom for the upright; He is a shield to those who walk uprightly;

He guards the paths of justice, and preserves the way of His saints. Then you will understand righteousness and justice, equity and every good path.

When wisdom enters your heart, and knowledge is pleasant to your soul, discretion will preserve you, understanding will keep you.

To deliver you from the way of evil, from the man who speaks perverse things.

Proverbs 7:24-27 Now therefore, listen to Me, My children; pay attention to the words of My mouth: Do not let your heart turn aside...Her house is the way to hell.

Proverbs 10:31-32 The mouth of the righteous brings forth wisdom, but the perverse tongue will be cut out. The lips of the righteous know what is acceptable, but the mouth of the wicked what is perverse.

Proverbs 11:13   A talebearer reveals secrets, but he who is of a faithful spirit conceals a matter.

Proverbs 13:3   He who guards his mouth preserves his life, but he who opens wide his lips shall have destruction.

Proverbs 15:2, 4, 7   The tongue of the wise uses knowledge rightly, but the mouth of fools pours forth foolishness.

Proverbs 3:19   The Lord by wisdom founded the earth; by understanding established the heavens;

Micah 2:7d   Do not My words do good to him who walks uprightly?

Micah 7:5c   Guard the doors of your mouth.

Deuteronomy 5:28-30   Then the Lord heard the voice of your words when you spoke to me, and the Lord said to me: 'I have heard the voice of the words of this people which they have spoken to you. They are right in all they have spoken. Oh that they had such a heart in them that they would fear Me and always keep My commandments, that it might be well with them and their children forever! Go and say to them, "Return to your tents."

Psalms1:1-3   Blessed is the man that walks not in the counsel of the ungodly. Nor stands in the presence of evil. Nor sits in the seat of the scornful. But his delight is in the law of the Lord. He meditates on it day and night. He shall bring forth his fruit in season, his leaf shall not wither and whatever he does shall prosper.

Proverbs 15:4   A wholesome tongue is a tree of life, but perverseness in it breaks the spirit.

Deuteronomy 12:28   Observe and obey all these words which I command you, that it may go well with you and your children after you forever, when you do what is good and right in the sight of the Lord your God.

Proverbs 30:5   Every word of God is pure; He is a shield to those who put their trust in Him.

Ecclesiastes 5:2   Do not be rash with your mouth, and let not your heart utter any

-thing hastily before God. For God is in Heaven, and you on earth, therefore, let your words be few.

Isaiah 40:8   The grass withers, the flower fades, But the word of our God stands forever.

Deuteronomy 28:58-59   If you do not carefully observe all the words of this law that are written in this book, that you may fear this glorious and awesome name, THE LORD YOUR GOD, *then the LORD will bring upon you and your descendants extraordinary plagues, great and prolonged plagues and serious and prolonged sicknesses.*

Thank You Jesus!

1 Kings 17:1 [*Elijah Proclaims a Drought*]
And Elijah the Tishbite, of the inhabitants of Gilead, said to Ahab, "As the LORD God of Israel lives, before whom I stand, there shall not be dew nor rain these years, except at my word."
1 Kings 17 (Whole Chapter)

Matthew 12:37 For by your words you will be justified and by your words you will be condemned.

Genesis 30:25-43 So my righteousness will answer for me in time to come, when the subject of my wages comes before you: every one that *is* not speckled and spotted among the goats, and brown among the lambs, will be considered stolen, if *It is* with me." And Laban said, "Oh, that it were <u>according to your word!</u>"

Exodus 8:10   So he said, "Tomorrow." And he said, "Let it be <u>according to your word</u>, that you may know that there is no one like the LORD our God. Exodus 8:9-11 (in Context) Exodus 8 (Whole Chapter)

Numbers 14:20   Then the LORD said: "I have pardoned, <u>according to your word</u>; Numbers 14:19-21 (in Context) Numbers 14 (Whole Chapter)

Deuteronomy 5:28   "Then the LORD heard the <u>voice of your words</u> when you spoke to

The Importance of The Armor

    I think that, as Christians, so many of us do not take advantage of putting on the armor. It's like having an outfit that you like but don't feel that it is stylish any more. It's folded up on the shelf or hanging in the back of the closet. When you take it out and shake it, putting on each piece carefully, you see that you still look good and it fits you like a glove.

    I envision the armor (outfit) glowing. You walk down the street with your head held high, confident in your relationship with God. You feel like you are floating above the ground. The devil sees you coming and runs the other way, saying, " Aw, man, they remembered to put it *on!*"

                                                     AJ

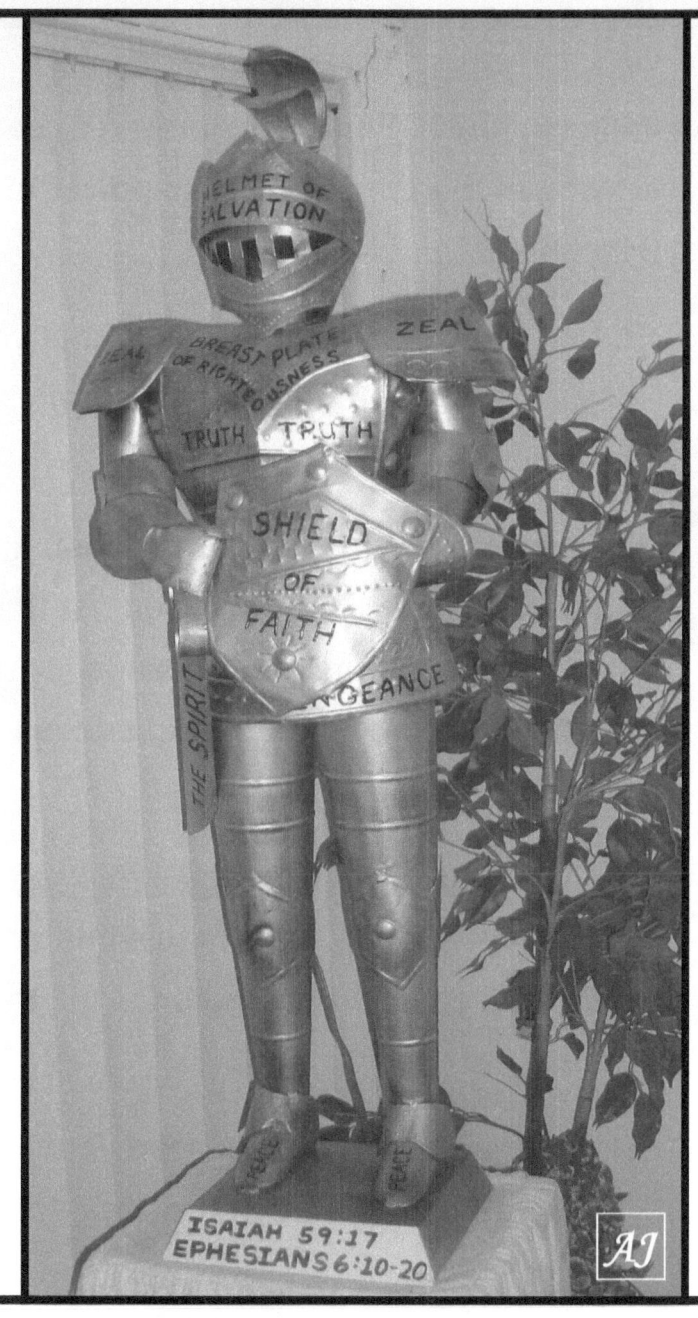

Suit of armor on display at Cherry Street Church of God

Ephesians 6:10-20 Finally my brethren, be strong in the Lord and in the power of His might.

Put on the whole armor of God, that you may be able to stand against the wiles of the devil.

For we do not wrestle against flesh and blood, but against powers, against the rulers of the darkness of this age, against spiritual hosts of wickedness in the heavenly places.

Therefore take up the whole armor of God, that you may be able to withstand in the evil day, and having done all, to stand,

Stand therefore, having girded your waist with truth, having put on the breastplate

<u>of righteousness,</u>

And having shod your feet with the preparation of the <u>gospel of peace</u>;

Above all, taking the <u>shield of faith </u>with which you will be able to quench all the fiery darts of the wicked one.

And take the <u>helmet of salvation</u>, and the <u>sword of the Spirit</u>, which is the ***<u>word of God;</u>***

Praying always with all prayer and supplication in the Spirit, being watchful to this end with all perseverance and supplication for all the saints…

Isaiah 59:17 For He put on <u>righteous</u>ness as a breastplate, and a <u>helmet of salvation</u> on His head; He put on the <u>garments of vengeance</u> for clothing, and was clad with <u>zeal as a cloak</u>.

Proverbs 15:4   A wholesome tongue is a tree of life, but perverseness in it breaks the spirit. The lips of the wise disperse knowledge, but the heart of the fool does not do so.

Proverbs 15:23   A man has joy by the answer of his mouth, and a word spoken in due season, how good it is!

Proverbs 15: 26   The heart of the righteous studies how to answer, but the mouth of the wicked pours forth evil.

Proverbs 18:20-21   Death and Life are in the power of the tongue.

Proverbs 21:23   Whoever guards his mouth and tongue keeps his soul from troubles.

Proverbs 16: 24   Pleasant words are like a honeycomb, sweetness to the soul and health to the bones.

Mark 16:17   And these signs shall follow those who believe: In My name they will cast out demons; they will speak with new tongues; They will take up serpents; And if they drink anything deadly, it will by no means hurt them; they will lay hands on the sick and they will recover.

Proverbs 15:28   The heart of the righteous studies how to answer, but the mouth of the wicked pours forth evil.

Proverbs 16:23-24   The heart of the wise teaches his mouth, and adds learning to his lips.

Proverbs 16: 20-24   He who heeds the word wisely will find good,   And whoever trusts in the LORD, happy *is* he.
The wise in heart will be called prudent, And sweetness of the lips increases learning.

Proverbs 16:22 Understanding *is* a wellspring of life to him who has it. But the correction of fools *is* folly. The heart of the wise teaches his mouth, and adds learning to his lips. Pleasant words are like a honeycomb, sweetness to the soul and health to the bones.

Proverbs 22:17-20 Incline your ear and hear the words of the wise, and apply your heart to My knowledge; for it is a pleasant thing if you keep them within you; Let them all be fixed upon your lips, so that your trust may be in the Lord.

Proverbs 23:7 For as he thinks in his heart, so is he.

Proverbs 25:11-12 A word fitly spoken is like apples of gold in settings of silver,

Like an earring of gold and an ornament of fine gold is a wise rebuke to an obedient ear.

Proverbs 12:14,17,19   A man will be satisfied with good by the fruit of his mouth. He who speaks truth declares righteousness The truthful lip shall be established for ever.

Proverbs 6:2 You are snared by the words of your mouth. Your are taken by the words of your mouth.

Matthew 12:36   But I say to you that for every idle word men may speak, they will give account of it in the day of judgment.

Proverbs 6:16   These six things the Lord hates, yes, seven are an abomination to Him: A Proud look, <u>A lying tongue</u>, Hands that shed innocent blood, A heart that devises wicked plans, Feet that are swift in running to evil, <u>A false witness who speaks lies,</u> And one who sows <u>discord</u> among brethren.   <u>(gossiping)</u>
My son, keep your father's command; And do not forsake the law of your mother.
Bind them continually on your heart; Tie them around your neck.
When you roam, they will lead you; When you sleep, they will keep you; And when you awake, they will speak with you.
For the commandment is a lamp, and the Law a light;

Blessed and Cursed

Ж

The Power of What We Say

And blessings will rain down ...

Blessing and cursing. God made this process so simple. Speaking. How hard is that? The word of God gives so many examples of both. Every time, it was just a matter of what was said.

Fathers were to bless their children before they died or before the children left home. Heroes spoke of what they would accomplish. Villains always spoke of what they thought they could do.

We do ourselves and others a grave disservice by speaking negative things over our situations, families, resources and lives.

We must practice positive confession. When we catch ourselves saying negative things, we should stop right then, repent of it and replace it with the word of God.

God has a blessing for every circumstance.

Genesis 49:1—27 And Jacob called his sons and said, 'Gather together that I may tell you what shall befall you in the last days.'

"Gather together and hear, you sons of Jacob, and listen to Israel your father: (God changed Jacob's name from "supplanter/trickster" to Israel, "prince")

"Reuben, you are my firstborn, my might and the beginning of my strength, the excellency of dignity and the excellency of power. Unstable as water, you shall not excel, because you went up to your father's bed; then you defiled it—he went up to my couch."   (Genesis 35:22)

"<u>Simeon and Levi</u> are brothers; instruments of cruelty are in their dwelling place. Let not my soul enter their council; Let not my honor be united to their assembly; for in their anger they slew a man, and in their self-will they hamstrung an ox. Cursed be their anger, for it is fierce; and their wrath, for it is cruel! I will divide them in Jacob and scatter them in Israel." (Genesis 34:25)

"<u>Judah</u>, you are he whom your brothers shall praise; your hand shall be on the neck of your enemies; Your father's children shall bow down before you. Judah is a lion's whelp; from the prey, my son, you have gone up. He bows down, he lies down as a lion; and as a lion, who shall rouse him? The scepter shall not depart from Judah, nor a lawgiver from between his feet, until Shiloh comes; and to him shall be the obedience of the people. Binding his donkey to the vine, and his donkey's colt to the choice vine. He washed his garments in wine, and his clothes in the blood of grapes. His eyes are darker than wine and his teeth are whiter than milk.   (Ruler?)

Zebulun shall dwell by the haven of the sea; he shall become a haven for ships, and his border shall adjoin Sidon. (Fleet owner?)

Issachar is a strong donkey, lying down between two burdens; he saw that rest was good, and that the land was pleasant; he bowed his shoulder to the burden, and became a band of slaves.

Dan shall judge his people as one of the tribes of Israel. Dan shall be a serpent by the way, a viper by the path, that bites the horse's heels so that its rider shall fall backward. I have waited for your salvation, O Lord! (Judge?)

Gad, a troop shall tramp upon him, but he shall triumph at last. (Warrior?)

Bread from Asher shall be rich, and he shall yield royal dainties. (Baker?)

Naphtali is a deer let loose; he uses beautiful words. (Writer/Poet?)

Joseph is a fruitful bough, a fruitful bough by a well; His branches run over the wall. The archers have bitterly grieved him. Shot at him and hated him. But his bow remained in strength.

And the arms of his hands were made strong by the hands of the Mighty God of Jacob. (From there is the Shepherd, the Stone of Israel), by the God of your father who will help you, and by the Almighty who will bless you with blessings of heaven above. Blessings of the deep that lies beneath, blessings of the breasts and of the womb. The blessings of your father have exceeded the blessings of my ancestors, up to the utmost bound of the everlasting hills. They shall be on the head of Joseph, and on the crown of the head of him who was separate from his brothers.   (rescuer of his people)

"<u>Benjamin</u> is a ravening wolf; in the morning he shall devour the prey, and at night he shall divide the spoil."
(hunter?)

All these are the twelve tribes of Israel, and this is what their father spoke to them. And he blessed each one according to his own blessing.

(Individually and specific to each one's character as he knew them)

Banners of the Twelve Tribes of Israel

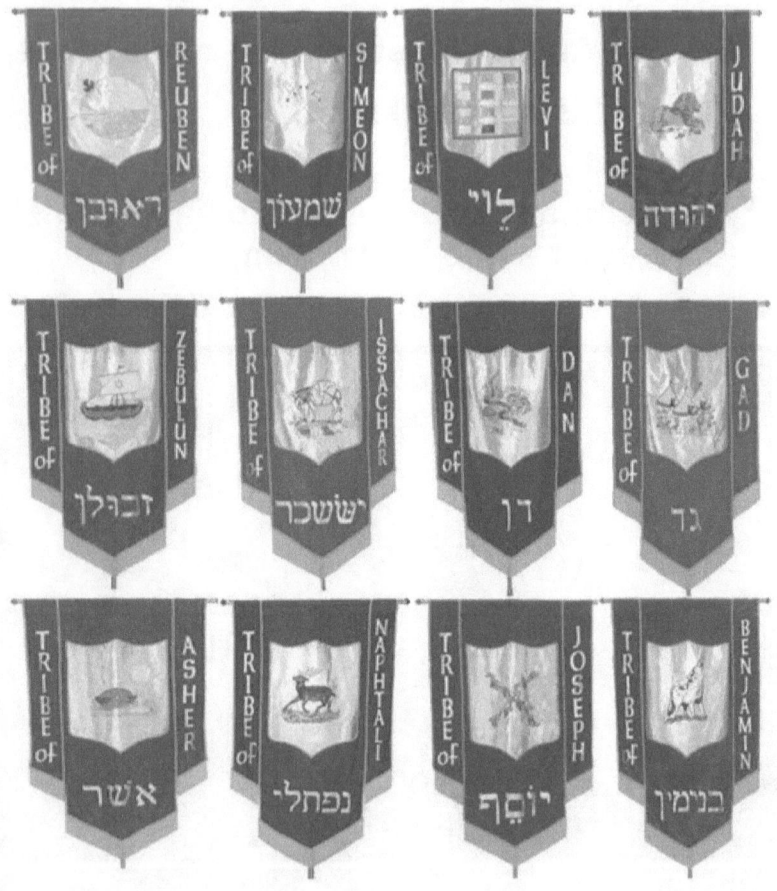

http://banahtorah.blogspot.com/2006/07/12-tribes-of-israel-banners.html

Genesis 48:11, 15   And Israel said to Joseph, "I had not thought to see your face; but in fact, God has shown me your offspring!"

And he blessed Joseph, and said: God, before whom my fathers Abraham and Isaac walked,

The God who has fed me all my life long to this day,

The angel who has redeemed me from all evil, bless the lads (Joseph's sons Ephraim and Manasseh),

Banners of Joseph's Son's Tribes

Deuteronomy 5:28 and the LORD said to me: 'I have heard the voice of the <u>words of this people</u> which they have spoken to you. They are right in all that they have spoken. Deuteronomy 5:27-29 (in Context) Deuteronomy 5 (Whole Chapter)

Daniel 10:12 Then he said to me, "Do not fear, Daniel, for from the first day that you set your heart to understand, and to humble yourself before your God, <u>your words were heard; and I have come because of your words</u>. Daniel 10:11-13 (in Context) Daniel 10 (Whole Chapter)

Hebrews 11:1 Now faith is the substance of things hoped for, the evidence of things not seen.

Hebrews 11:6 But without faith, it is impossible to please Him, for he who comes to

God must believe that He is, and that He is a rewarder of those who diligently seek Him.

Romans 3:5 For what if some did not believe? Will their unbelief make the faithfulness of God of no effect? Certainly not! Indeed, let God be true but every man a liar. As it is written: "That you may be justified in your words, and may overcome when you are judged."

Faith Works

Ж

Only Believe

I added these stories to confirm my belief that, what you say, in faith, will come to pass, if you live in agreement with God's words.

Romans 4: 17, 20-22 As it is written, (I have made you a father of many nations,) in the presence of him whom he believed, even God, who gives life to the dead, and calls those things which do not exist as though they did.

He did not waver at the promise of God through unbelief; but was strengthened in faith, giving glory to God;

And being fully convinced that, what He had promised, He was also able to perform.

And therefore it was accounted to him for righteousness.

Revelations 12:11

And they overcame him by the blood of the Lamb and the word of their testimony and they did not love their lives to the death.

Isaiah 53:5   But He was wounded for our transgresssions; He was bruised for our iniquities. The chastisement of our peace was upon Him, and with His stripes we are healed

53:11   He shall see of the travail of His soul, and shall be satisfied. By His knowledge shall my righteous Servant justify many, for He shall bear their iniquities.

53:12   And He was numbered with the transgressors; and He bore the sin of many, and made intercession for the transgressors.

Geoffrey

I visited our son once in New York City; the only time that we could *kind of* coordinate our vacations. He was upset that mine came the week before his payday. I had enough to get there and back. I told him that I was coming to visit him and not to worry about taking me anywhere. I would be able to see the Empire State Building and the Statue of Liberty. He said there was so much more to see, but it was expensive. I tried to reassure him but was getting nowhere.

Before I went to see him, I asked God to show Himself to Geoff, who had attended philosophy classes at the university and was convinced that there were things he just didn't believe so easily any more.

While he was furiously looking on his computer for free things to show me, I was walking around his apartment praying and anointing doors and windows.

I then put oil on my hand and went and rubbed his head while he was on the computer muttering. He relaxed instantaneously and said that he wanted to take me to lunch at a place that served the *best* jerk chicken.

He then said that it was lunch time and we probably wouldn't get a parking place. I told him that we would. He said, "This is New York, you just don't know." I said again that we would. He shook his head and went toward the door.

We went through traffic at, what seemed to me, breakneck speed, and he said, "This is New York, that's how you have to drive; plus

I need to find a parking space." I told him again, not to worry. He shook his head again.

When we got to the restaurant there was a parking space across the street from it. It had a broken meter. The meter maid was on the corner from the restaurant. I put a note on the meter saying that it didn't work. Geoff said that didn't matter, we would get a ticket. I said, "No, we won't. He said, "This is New York, you don't know." We went to an excellent lunch. When we came back, the meter maid had not moved from where she was, and we went on our way.

I spent the week with him and his family. We had a wonderful time together, visiting museums and looking at the sights.

When it was time for me to leave, Geoff said, "You are going to be here tomorrow if we don't hurry up." I told him that we had to pray first. He said again that I would miss the train. I insisted that we pray. His wife, the two kids and I, held hands. Their dog sat quietly in the middle of the circle. I prayed and Geoff said again that I would miss the train. I said I wouldn't. He said, "This is New York!

    We once again raced through the streets. We got to the train 25 minutes late . Geoff said, "We might as well go home." I said it was ok. We got out of the car. While he was getting the luggage out of the trunk, a woman came to the door of the station, about a hundred feet away, and said, "Relax, take your time, they are waiting for you." We all looked at each other.

    When we got inside, there was a woman at the top of the escalator who repeated the phrase. At the base of the escalator, a man said the same thing. From the front of the train, until the door where I was to board, were three more people greeting me. At the door was the conductor, who said, "Welcome, we've been waiting." I hugged Geoff and said, "You see?" He hugged me tightly and said, "Yeah, Ma, I see." As soon as I got on the train and settled, it pulled away from the station.

God gave me the assurance that He would show Himself to Geoff. He gave me the peace to confirm that, in every statement. He sent His angels to greet me. Geoff's wife kept saying, "This is New York. That couldn't happen. It didn't happen!!!"

When Geoff was a child, he was scheduled for surgery twice to remove tumors. Both times, the day of surgery, the tumors were gone.

Danielle

Our daughter Danielle was 18 months old when she had a terrible accident.

I was coming down with the flu that had my husband sick for a week. He was still feeling a little under the weather. He decided to go to the Father's Day dinner at my aunt's house where our grandfather was being honored. I had prepared a huge mug of tea for myself and had gone to wake my husband from his nap so he could go to the dinner. The children were at the table eating lunch.

When I was almost at the kitchen door, (it was as if it were in slow motion), I saw the tea coming down on Danielle. It splashed on her chest, arm, neck and face. She fell forward into it on the floor and the remainder, with the sugar in it, dripped on her back.

I had put a sweater on her earlier so she could play on the back porch. She had a shirt and that sweater on. When they were removed, her skin came off with them.

I was splashing cold water on her and she was, naturally, screaming her lungs out. Johnny was trying to get Geoff ready so we could get to the hospital.

Johnny ran the light while I tried to hold her hands to keep her from clawing at herself. As soon as we got to the hospital, she was whisked away. Johnny went to call the family, for them to pray. Danielle went to sleep and did not wake up while they pulled the remaining burnt skin off of her. She did not wake the entire time. She had third degree burns over twenty percent of her body.

When they finished wrapping her chest, neck and head, her arm was sticking straight out to the side because of all the bandages.

They let us take her home because she was asleep. They thought we would have to bring her back when she woke up. She slept until eleven o'clock that night and woke to ask for an apple and went back to sleep.

Danielle had a speech problem, so people were always asking me what she had said. Grandma called the next day to see how Dani was doing. She could hear her clearly singing, "Yes, Jesus Loves Me."

When we took Dani to the hospital to have the bandages changed later that day, she only cried when they removed the one from her back; it was the deepest and had seeped so the bandages had stuck.

There was a different doctor on duty now. He was looking at her records from the day before and thought they were either the wrong records or this was the wrong child. The same male nurse was back and assured the doctor that he recognized the mother, so it had to be the same kid.

There, under the bandages, was new skin. It was shaped like hands. One on each side facing each other. It was as if God was holding her.

The only evidence of her ordeal is a small scar under her chin shaped like a cross. Danielle is now an MD herself. She works at a whole-person psychiatric hospital, where she is a psychiatrist. She is the Chief Medical Officer.

Dani has a young son who she has shared her faith with. He calls and asks for prayer, just like she did when she was a child. They ask for prayer believing that God will answer. He always does.

When Geoffrey and Danielle were chidren, we took them to church from the age of one week . What they learned in Sunday School, they believed wholeheartedly.

Whenever I was ill, they would drop to their knees so fast that I was afraid that they would break their knees. Without fail, I would get better right away.

The Bible says that except we become as little children, we will not please Him. Whatever you tell a child, they will believe it until you prove that what you said was a lie.

God is not a man that He should lie. No need to lie, He can accomplish everything that He says.

Johnny

My husband, Johnny, had been complaining of abdominal pain for some time. He had visited his doctor on a few occasions and was told that he had gall bladder trouble. He was given medication for it. He felt no better.

He was lying down and I had tried to wake him. He was burning with fever. When we got to the hospital, his temperature was 106. He was examined and told that his appendix had ruptured. He was scheduled for surgery immediately.

I called family and they started praying. The surgery went well. Doctors were amazed because the appendix had ruptured three times. All the poison was encased in a membrane which kept it from killing him.

The next day, he was up and walking around. He was released from the hospital in two days and went back to his regular routine.

On another occasion, Johnny was experiencing back pain. He was given a pain killer and a muscle relaxant. Neither worked. He was sent to a neurologist who did an MRI which showed a tumor inside his spine. We were told that the operation that he needed could leave him paralyzed. The doctor explained that because of where the tumor was, it could happen with or without surgery.

The surgery was a success.

Angela

    I was taking chemo therapy in an effort to control multiple sclerosis symptoms. I had taken my fourth treatment and had not gotten ill or had any symptoms. Until this one. I was nauseated and dizzy. I was like that for a week. I had not been able to eat. My husband brought me a sandwich. I ate a couple of bites and, feeling worse, decided to go to bed.

    On my way to bed, I called my husband to tell him that I was having trouble walking. He said that he was coming. Before he could get to me, I hit the floor. I couldn't get up, couldn't talk, I was foaming at the mouth, and I was soaked with a cold sweat. My husband was trying to help me up, unsuccessfully. I finally was able to say, "Help!" He called the ambulance.

I found out, the next day, that I had experienced an ischemic stroke. I initially had weakness and pain on the left side of my body. I was released from the hospital three days later about five o'clock pm. By seven o'clock, I was back with the second stroke.

After prayer and rehab, I have none of the symptoms. I can lift 170 lbs. on the leg press machine.

Along with the strokes, I was diagnosed with multiple sclerosis 35 years ago. I was told 34 years ago that I would be bedridden. I was even supposed to be sent away to "learn how to be disabled."

Surprise! I'm still kickin'. I take a self defense class. I even learned how to break a board !

AJ

The Consequences of Unbelief

Ж

What It Does To Us

Mark 8:36–38 "For what will it profit a man if he gains the whole world and loses his own soul?

Or what will a man give in exchange for his soul?

For whoever is ashamed of Me and My words in this adulterous and sinful generation, of him the Son of Man also will be ashamed when he comes in the glory of His Father with the holy angels."

Matthew 10:33 "But whoever denies Me before men, him I will also deny before My Father who is in Heaven."

2 Timothy 2:12 If we endure, we shall also reign with Him. If we deny Him, He also will deny us.

John 3:18-20   He who believes is not condemned; but he who does not believe is condemned already, because he has not believed in the name of the only begotten Son."

And this is the condemnation, that the light has come into the world, and men loved darkness rather than light, because their deeds were evil.

Leviticus 19:12   And you shall not swear by My name falsely, nor shall you profane the name of your God: I am the LORD.
Leviticus 19:11-13 (in Context)
Leviticus 19 (Whole Chapter)

Deuteronomy 5:11   'You shall not take the name of the LORD your God in vain, for the LORD will not hold him guiltless who takes His name in vain.

Deuteronomy 18:20   But the prophet who presumes to speak a word in My name, which I have not commanded him to speak, or who speaks in the name of other gods, that prophet shall die.

Hebrews 3:11-13   So I swore in my wrath, "They shall not enter My rest." Beware, Brethren lest there be in any of you an evil heart of unbelief in departing from the living God; but exhort one another daily while it is called "Today", lest any of you be hardened through the deceitfulness of sin.

Hebrews 3:18   And to whom did He swear that they would not enter into His rest, but to those who did not obey? So we see that they could not enter in because of unbelief.

Romans 11:19-22   You will say then, "Branches were broken off, that I may be grafted in." Well said. Because of unbelief they were broken off, and you stand by faith. Do not be haughty, but fear. For if God did not spare the natural branches, He may not spare you either. Therefore consider the goodness and severity of God: on those who fell, severity; but toward you, goodness, if you continue in *His* goodness. Other wise you also will be cut off.

    Why should just anyone enjoy God's blessings? You say that, if He is a loving God, everyone should get blessed. We are, when we accept His Son as our Savior. He shed His blood for that purpose. It was for nothing if we don't have to do our part. God forbid, but if I lost a child because of anyone, I would *own* them.

HE IS

He is Father, Son, and Holy Spirit.
He is The Word and I want to hear it.
I will hide it in my heart that I might not sin against Him.
Not change like the wind at *my* every whim.
I want to show Him in every thought word and deed;
An example of life lived for Him as He supplies my every need.
He's been very patient with me; *my* child could not ask for more.
Behold, He stands and knocks, I need only open the door.
As humans, we are stubborn and rebellious as a goat.
But of all our promises, He already wrote.
He often grows weary and wonders why it takes so long.
For on the cross He took from us everything that was wrong.
Sin is a three letter word and we all have committed them;
We just have to repent and turn around-- back to Him.
He stands before us with His arms opened wide.
Against the enemy, He will always take our side.
So let's go home---Prodigal child no more to roam.

Redeemed By His Blood

Ж

Through His Word

From the beginning of time, He sat at the right hand of God. He loved looking upon Their creations. Man being the greatest.

In short time, man forgot who God was. He listened to the whisperings of satan. Jesus could feel the Father growing more and more agitated. God said, "I ought to just destroy them all."

"But Father, they aren't all evil. See, some are praying and worshiping you right now."

Okay, I won't get rid of all of them, but I am tired of this. They don't appreciate my protection and blessings."

"I have searched Heaven for a sacrifice and can find none. There is no redemption of sin without a blood sacrifice. It would take a lot of blood to cover all these sins."

Jesus: Then make me a body and I will go.

God: No, Son, they won't appreciate it.

Jesus: It's ok, I'll go.

God: They'll betray you.

Jesus: I'll go.

God: They will lie on you.

Jesus: I'll go.

God: They'll desert you.

Jesus: I'll go.

God: Are you sure?

Jesus: Yes, Father, I know their faults but I love them, make me a body.

    God sent His Holy Spirit to impregnate a virgin girl so that the birth would be pure. She was engaged to a young man who had decided to put her away to spare them the embarrassment. The angel of the Lord came to him and told him that the baby she was carrying was conceived by the Holy Ghost.

This baby was our Lord and Savior, Jesus Christ. He lived an exemplary life that taught us how to love, how to live, how to stand against the wiles of the devil. He was betrayed as God said He would. He was lied on, He was deserted, He was tortured and brutalized, then crucified. His crucifixion was worse than any other. He was carrying the sins of the entire world for all generations. His pain was worse—His suffering so terrible that God had to turn His back to keep from looking at it. If He had looked, He probably would have destroyed everyone. Jesus shed the required blood for the remission of sins. God let Him do it because Christ volunteered to do it, but it fulfilled the scripture;

For God so loved the world that He gave His only begotten Son that <u>whosoever</u> believes in Him should not perish but have everlasting life. St. John 3:16

Throughout history, people have fought and died during their arguments over who crucified and killed Jesus. The absolute truth is that it doesn't matter *who* did it. Without His death and resurrection we would all be lost for eternity.

𝒜𝒥

John 3:17   For God did not send His Son into the world to condemn the world, but that the world through Him might be <u>saved</u>.

2 Corinthians 7:10   For Godly sorrow produces repentance leading to salvation not to be regretted, but the sorrow of the world produces death.

2 Peter 3:9   The Lord is not slack concerning his promise, as some count slackness, but is longsuffering toward us, not willing that any should perish but that all should come to <u>repentance</u>.

Philippians 2:12   Therefore, my beloved, as you have always obeyed, not as in my presence only, but now much more in my absence, work out your own <u>salvation</u> with fear and trembling.

1 Thessalonians 5:9   For God did not appoint us to wrath, but to obtain <u>salvation</u>.

Romans 10:8-10   But what does it say? "The word is near you, in your mouth and in your heart" (that is, the word of faith which we preach): that if you confess with your mouth the Lord Jesus and believe in your heart that God has raised Him from the dead, you will be <u>saved</u>. For with the heart one believes unto <u>righteousness</u>, and with the mouth confession is made unto <u>salvation.</u>

Matthew 10:32   Therefore whoever confesses Me before men, him I will also confess before My Father who is in Heaven.

John 17:2-3 as You have given Him authority over all flesh, that He should give eternal life to as many as You have given Him. And this is eternal life, that they may know You, the only true God, and Jesus Christ whom You have sent.

Luke 12:8   And I say to you, whoever confesses Me before men, him the Son of Man also will confess before the angels of God.

Romans 8 There is therefore now no condemnation to those who are in Christ Jesus, who do not walk according to the flesh, but according to the Spirit.

For the law of the Spirit of life in Christ Jesus has made me free from the law of sin and death.

For what the law could not do in that it was weak through the flesh, God did by sending His own Son in the likeness of sinful flesh, on account of sin: He condemned sin in the flesh, that the righteous requirement of the law might be fulfilled in us who do not walk according to the flesh but according to the Spirit.

For those who live according to the flesh set their minds on the things of the flesh,

but those who live according to the Spirit, the things of the Spirit.

For to be carnally minded is death, but to be spiritually minded is life and peace.

Because the carnal mind is enmity against God; for it is not subject to the law of God, nor indeed can be.

So then, those who are in the flesh cannot please God.

But you are not in the flesh but in the Spirit, if indeed the Spirit of God dwells in you. Now if anyone does not have the Spirit of Christ, he is not His.

And if Christ is in you, the body is dead because of sin, but the Spirit is life because of righteousness.

But if the Spirit of Him who raised Jesus from the dead dwells in you, He who raised Christ from the dead will also give life to your mortal bodies through His Spirit who dwells in you.   Romans 8

Christ Walking on the Water

Picture painted on the dining hall wall
of Cherry Street Church of God
of Erie, PA
in 1970 by the author

WORLD'S HIGHEST STATUE

CHRIST THE REDEEMER,

RIO DE JANEIRO, BRAZIL

Christ the Redeemer is a statue of Jesus Christ in Rio de Janeiro, Brazil, considered the largest art deco statue in the world. The statue stands 39.6 meters (130 ft) tall, including its 9.5 meter (31 ft) pedestal, and 30 meters (98 ft) wide. It weighs 635 tons (700 short tons), and is located at the peak of the 700 meters (2,300 ft) Corcovado mountain in the Tijuca Forest National Park overlooking the city. It is one of the tallest of its kind in the world. The statue has become an icon of Rio and Brazil. It is made of reinforced concrete and soapstone.

http://www.martmut.com/?plugin_calendar_month=03&plugin_calendar_year=2010&pr_content=49

Who This Works For

Ж

Who "Gets" It

Galatians 3:28   There is neither Jew nor Greek, there is neither slave nor free, there is neither male nor female; for <u>you are all one in Christ Jesus.</u>

Revelations 5:9   And "they sang a new song, saying: "You are worthy to take the scroll, and to open its seals; for you were slain, and have redeemed us to God by Your blood out of <u>every tribe and tongue and people and nation,</u> and have made us kings and priests to our God: and we shall reign on the earth."

Revelations 7:9-10   After these things I looked, and behold, a great multitude which no one could number, of <u>all nations, tribes, peoples, and tongues,</u> standing before the throne and before the Lamb, clothed with white robes, with palm branches in their hands, and crying out with a loud voice, saying, "Salvation *belongs* to our God who sits on the throne, and to the Lamb!"

Daniel 7:14   Then to Him was given dominion and glory and a kingdom, that <u>all peoples nations, and languages</u> should serve Him. His dominion is an everlasting dominion, which shall not pass away, and His kingdom the one which shall not be destroyed.

Mark 11:17   Then He taught, saying to them, "It is written, 'My house shall be called a house of prayer <u>for all nations</u>? But you have made it a den of thieves.' "

Titus 2:11   For the grace of God that brings salvation has appeared to <u>all men</u>.

Revelation 14:6   Then I saw another angel flying in the midst of heaven, having the everlasting gospel to preach to those who dwell on the earth—<u>to every nation, tribe, tongue, and people</u>

Daniel 4:1   Nebuchadnezzar the king,
To all <u>peoples, nations, and languages</u>
that dwell in <u>all the earth</u>:
Peace be multiplied to you.

Believers, regardless of what color Adam and Eve were, we all started there. Maybe God didn't stop in the Garden of Eden but kept creating in other parts of the world. The dust of the earth comes in all colors; from the whitest white to the blackest black and everything in between. We are children of God. He loves us ALL. Hallelujah!

AJ

How To Receive

Ж

What About Me?

Acts 16:30   And he brought them out and said, "Sir, what must I do to be <u>saved</u>?"

So they said, "Believe on the Lord Jesus Christ, and you will be <u>saved</u>, you and your household."

1 John 1:9   If we confess our sins, He is faithful and just to forgive us our sins and to <u>cleanse</u> us from all unrighteousness.

Acts 3:19   Repent therefore and be <u>converted</u>, that your sins may be blotted out, so that times of refreshing may come from the presence of the Lord.

Acts 4:12   Nor is there <u>salvation</u> in any other, for there is no other name under heaven given among men by which we must be saved."   Acts 4:11-13 (in Context)   Acts 4 (Whole Chapter)

1 John 4:15-16   Whoever confesses that Jesus is the son of God, God abides in him, and He in God. And we have known and believed the love that God has for us. God is love, and he who abides in love <u>abides</u> in God, and God in him.

Ephesians 2:8   For by grace you have been <u>saved</u> through faith, and that not of ourselves; it is the gift of God.

Romans 10:1,9; 14:11   Brethren, my heart's desire and prayer to God for Israel is that they may be <u>saved</u>.

For I bear them witness that they have a zeal for God, but not according to knowledge.

For they being ignorant of God's righteousness, have not submitted to the righteousness of God.

For Christ is the end of the law for righteousness to everyone that believes.

For Moses writes about the <u>righteousness</u> which is of the law. "The man who does those things shall live by them."

Romans 10:10 For with the *heart* one believes unto <u>righteousness</u>, and with the *mouth* confession is made unto <u>salvation</u>.
Romans 10:9-11 in Context)
Romans 10 (Whole Chapter)

2 Corinthians 7:10 For godly sorrow produces <u>repentance leading to salvation</u>, not to be regretted; but the sorrow of the world produces death. 2 Corinthians 7:9-11 (in Context) 2 Corinthians 7 (Whole Chapter)

1 Thessalonians 5:9 For God did not appoint us to wrath, but to obtain <u>salvation</u>

through our Lord Jesus Christ,
1 Thessalonians 5:8-10 (in Context)
1 Thessalonians 5 (Whole Chapter)

Ephesians 1:13 In Him you also trusted, after you heard the word of truth, the gospel of your salvation; in whom also, having believed, you were sealed with the Holy Spirit of promise,
Ephesians 1:12-14 (in Context)
Ephesians 1 (Whole Chapter)

Philippians 2:12 Therefore, my beloved, as you have always obeyed, not as in my presence only, but now much more in my absence, work out your own salvation with fear and trembling.
Philippians 2:11-13 (in Context)
Philippians 2 (Whole Chapter)

2 Timothy 2:10   Therefore I endure all things for the sake of the elect, that they also may obtain the <u>salvation</u> which is in Christ Jesus with eternal glory.
2 Timothy 2:9-11 (in Context)
2 Timothy 2 (Whole Chapter)

2 Timothy 3:15 And that from childhood you have known the Holy Scriptures, which are able to make you wise for <u>salvation</u> through faith which is in Christ Jesus.
2 Timothy 3:14-16 (in Context)

Titus 2:11 For the grace of God that brings <u>salvation</u> has appeared to all men,
Titus 2:10-12 (in Context)
Titus 2 (Whole Chapter)

Hebrews 5:9   And having been perfected, He became the author of eternal <u>salvation</u> to all who obey Him,
>Hebrews 5:8-10 (in Context)
>Hebrews 5 (Whole Chapter)

Hebrews 9:28   So Christ was offered once to bear the sins of many. To those who eagerly wait for Him He will appear a second time, apart from sin, for <u>salvation.</u>   Hebrews 9:27-28 (in Context)
>Hebrews 9 (Whole Chapter)

Revelation 19:1 After these things I heard a loud voice of a great multitude in heaven, saying, "Alleluia! <u>Salvation</u> and glory and honor and power belong to the Lord our God!
>Revelation 19:1-3 (in Context)
>Revelation 19 (Whole Chapter)

1 Thessalonians 5:9   For God did not appoint us to wrath, but to obtain <u>salvation</u> through our Lord Jesus Christ.

Hebrews 2:10   For it was fitting for Him, for whom are all things, in bringing many sons to glory, to make the captain of their <u>salvation</u> perfect through sufferings.

Hebrews 5:9   And having been perfected, He became the author of eternal <u>salvation</u> to all who obey Him.

Hebrews 9:28   So Christ was offered once to bear the sins of many. To those who eagerly wait for Him, He will appear a second time, apart from sin, for <u>salvation</u>.

2 Samuel 22:3   The God of my strength, in whom I will trust; my shield and the horn

of my salvation, my stronghold and my refuge, my Savior, You save me from violence.

2 Samuel 22:36   You have also given me the shield of Your salvation, Your gentleness has made me great.

1 Chronicles 16:23   Sing to the Lord, all the earth, proclaim the good news of His salvation from day to day.

What Now?

Ж

Where Do I Go From Here?

God not only desires and expects great things for us, but *from* us, as His children. He has supplied us with everything we need to do His will. He has given us the instruction manual (Bible) to operate in every situation and under all circumstances. There is not one thing that we will encounter in this present day that has not been encountered in Biblical times. "There is nothing new under the sun." The phrase, "that's old school" has been voiced by every generation. The problem with that is, so many "old school" things that worked have been cast aside, leaving more problems in their wake. Also leaving no "new school" solutions. We often hear, 'why does this keep happening to me?' Are you accepting advice from someone who is in worse shape than you? The "old" saying is 'if you keep on doing what you've always done, you will keep on gettin' what you always got.' Change one thing in your life.

Accepting Christ as your personal Savior is just the beginning. We are fallible human beings. We go through so many experiences in our lives. We relish the positive and regret the negative. Asking God to give you the Holy Spirit is a powerful decision. It is the infilling of the Holy Spirit that helps you get through each day without battling for your sanity, and without battling other people.

AJ

Luke 11:13 If you then, being evil, know how to give good gifts to your children, how much more will your heavenly Father give the Holy Spirit to those who ask Him!" <u>Luke 11:12-14</u> (in Context)

Galatians 5:22 But the fruit of the Spirit is love, joy, peace, longsuffering, kindness,

goodness, faithfulness,
Galatians 5:21-23 (in Context)
Galatians 5 (Whole Chapter)

1 Corinthians 12:4-11 There are diversities of gifts, but the same Spirit. There are differences of ministries, but the same Lord. And there are diversities of activities, but it is the same God who works all in all. But the manifestation of the Spirit is given to each one for the profit *of all:* for to one is given the word of wisdom through the Spirit, to another the word of knowledge through the same Spirit, to another faith by the same Spirit, to another gifts of healings by the same Spirit, to another the working of miracles, to another prophecy, to another discerning of spirits, to another *different* kinds of tongues, to another the interpretation of tongues. But one and the same Spirit works all these things, distributing to each one individually as He wills.

Daniel 11:32   But the people who know their God shall be strong, and carry out great exploits.

Acts 2:38   Then Peter said to them, "Repent, and let everyone of you be baptized in the name of Jesus Christ for the remission of sins: and you shall receive the gift of the Holy Spirit.

2 Timothy 2:21   Therefore if anyone cleanses himself from the latter, he will be a vessel for honor, sanctified and useful for the Master, prepared for every good work.

Isaiah 61:1"The Spirit of the Lord GOD is upon Me, because the LORD has anointed Me To preach good tidings to the poor; He has sent Me to heal the brokenhearted, To proclaim liberty to the captives, And the opening of the prison to those who are bound; Isaiah 61 (Whole Chapter)

Matthew 10:27 Whatever I tell you in the dark, speak in the light.; and what you hear in the ear, preach in the housetops.

Mark 16:20 And they went out and preached everywhere, the Lord working with them and confirming the word through the accompanying signs. Amen.
Mark 16:19-21 (in Context)
Mark 16 (Whole Chapter)

Luke 7:22 Jesus answered and said to them, "Go and tell John the things you have seen and heard: that the blind see, the lame walk, the lepers are cleansed, the

deaf hear, the dead are raised, the poor have the gospel preached to them.
Luke 7: 21-23 (in context)
Luke 7   Whole Chapter

Luke 9:2   He sent them to preach the kingdom of God and to heal the sick. Luke 9:1-3 (in Context) Luke 9 (Whole Chapter)

Acts 28:31   preaching the kingdom of God and teaching the things which concern the Lord Jesus Christ with all confidence, no one forbidding him. (them)
Acts 28:30-31 (in Context)
Acts 28 (Whole Chapter)

Matthew 24:14 And this gospel of the kingdom will be preached in all the world as a witness to all the nations, and then the end will come. Matthew 24:13-15 (in Context) Matthew 24 (Whole Chapter)

God is a spirit. We must worship Him in spirit and truth. He is Father, Son, and Holy Spirit. All three are One. They are each God but He is "The" God.

Jesus is the Son. He was born of a virgin girl who was impregnated by the Holy Spirit. He was raised in the Hebrew culture, teaching in the synagogue, teaching on the mountainside, healing the sick, raising the dead, walking on water, vanishing and reappearing, transporting Himself from one place to another, and casting out demons. He lived on the earth until He was 33 and was crucified for our sins. Jesus sacrificed Himself for us. He intended that purpose before He came to Earth in the form of an infant. He knew He would die. Without the shedding of blood, there is no forgiveness of sins. He wasn't excited about it but knew it was necessary. The Father has the final say when Jesus comes again.

The Holy Spirit interprets for us. He tells God what we really mean to say in our hearts. If we speak in the Heavenly Language then the enemy does not know what we are saying and can't use our words against us.

We often say stupid things that the enemy throws in our faces and tells God, "See, I thought that they were such good Christians but II know you heard what they said.

The Holy Spirit makes us stronger spiritually, able to handle things that we couldn't before. He teaches us things that we were not spiritually mature enough to understand before. He is often who we call on now that Jesus went back to Heaven. We can call on any one or all three of Them at any time. They will respond.

The saying is "He may not come when you want Him but He's right on time." Just have faith, without which we cannot please God. Faith like little children who will believe whatever you say until you prove yourself wrong.

Epilogue

Perhaps it is because of the family that I was around for a short time. Perhaps it is because of something that is in me, but I have always known that there is a God. Maybe it was my childish hope that the God that I heard my grandparents talk about was real.

I did not grow up in an ideal situation but I was always saying that if He would get me out of this one thing or another, that I would do better.

Every time that I listened to that still small voice of God, I would do well, making the right decisions. But...when I looked away, looking for approval from others, I messed up.

God has at certain times given me very insightful and wise things to say but I would look to others. I would think that what I was about to say did not sound like me. Of course not, idiot, it's not you. In which case, the me that came out was always wrong.

Looking for the approval of others over God will *always* take you to places and situations that you will regret.

He is a jealous God who will not be put in second place or ignored. There are consequences. Stepping back from Him takes you out of the circle of protection that is before God. The enemy can make you eat any negative words or make you live in, any negative circumstances.

God can help if you repent of the words and replace the negative with *His* Word. Pray His word, speak His Word, and stand on His Word. It is, after all, the weapon that Christ used against satan. Matthew 4:3-9

>Christ in you the hope of glory.
>Colossians 1:27

Scripture References
and definitions

Tree not moved	Jeremiah 17:8; Ps 1:3
Not a man	Numbers 23:9
Dust of the earth	Genesis 2:7
Cattle on thousand hills	Psalm 50:10
Do not reward bad behaviors	
Go into the world	Mark 16:15
Submit to God	James 4:7
Washed in Blood	Revelations 7:14
All things new	2 Corinthians 5:17
Mind of Christ	1 Corinthians 2:1
In Christ	Romans 6:11
Joint Heir	Romans 8:7
Authority	Luke 9:1; 10:19
Weapons of warfare	2 Corinthians 10:4
More than a conqueror	Romans 8:37
Greater is He	1 John 4:4
Salt of the earth	Matthew 5:13
Sheep of His pasture	Psalm 100:3

Scripture References

Blessed and favored   Revelations 1:6
Jesus said we are *gods*   John 10:34
Image of God   Genesis 1:27
Overcome thru blood   Revelations 12:11
Strong in Lord   Ephesians 6:10
God in everything   Matthew 28:20
    Joshua 1:9
    2 Corinthians 5:5
    2 Timothy 2:21
Word will do God's will   Isaiah 55:11

Eat from the fruit   Proverbs 18:21
Abundance   Ephesians 3:20
Spirit and truth   John 4:23
These three are one   1 John 5:7,8
Teaching in synagogue   Matthew 4:13
    Matthew 9:35
Healing the sick, raising the dead, casting out demons, walking on water, disappearing
    Matthew 5:17; 7:22, 8:28-33; 8:59; 11;5; 14:22; 28:20 Mark 6:6; Luke 13:22; 21:37 John 8:59; 12:36

Nancy Walker
1922-1992

    Nancy Walker was an actress and comedian of stage, screen and television. Her career spanned five decades.

    She was also a director and musician who sang and played the drums. She released a couple of albums.

    She won a Tony, was nominated for eight Emmy's and won four Golden Globes.

    She guest appeared on many talk shows and sit-coms. She was a regular on: The Mary Tyler Moore Show—1970-73; McMillan and Wife—1971-76; Rhoda—1974-78; True Colors—1990-92.

    She was the face for Bounty paper towels (The quicker picker upper.) from 1970-1990.

www.ingramcontent.com/pod-product-compliance
Lightning Source LLC
LaVergne TN
LVHW091552060526
838200LV00036B/802